DANCING
WITH
ANGELS

DANCING WITH
ANGELS
The Journey Home

A Spiritual Tale
By Susan M. Hoskins

Integrity Press, Ltd.
Prairie Village, Kansas

First Edition, 1998

Published by
Integrity Press, Ltd.
P.O. Box 8277
Prairie Village, KS 66208

Printed in the United States of America

Typeset by Jill Ziegler
Illustrations by Dave Howard
Cover design by Jill Ziegler
Production by Jill Ziegler

Library of Congress Cataloging-in-Publication Data
Hoskins, Susan M.
        Dancing With Angels
catalog card number 98-070726
ISBN 0-9656581-2-0

Dedication

To Each of Us,
God's Angels in Training.

To Christopher, my Guide, and
Melanie Grace, my Guardian Angel.

To Rayna Horner,
Thank you for your wisdom and inspiration.
You are my teacher, my angel, my friend.

To Rev. Mary Omwake,
Bukeka Shoals, Jerome Johnson and
The Music Ministry of Unity Church of Overland Park,
Thank you for holding a higher vision as I walked
through the darkest hours of my own despair.

To ministers from all walks of life,
Your light illuminates the pathway home.

In July of 1996,

my well-ordered world was shattered

by a series of events totally out of my control.

Devastated by loss,

I turned to prayer and meditation for understanding.

My question was a simple one:

"Why did this happen, God?"

Dancing with Angels,

The Journey Home, was my answer.

*I*t was late one afternoon in early October. My day's work was finished. Random pages of my novel were locked away in a desk drawer. The computer was silent. Dinner was simmering on the stove. My husband and daughter were due home soon. Every chore on my list was completed. The beds were made. The laundry was finished. The house was orderly and quiet.

With a few minutes to spare, I meandered to the living room. I gazed out the picture window. The brilliant hues of autumn painted the landscape. The windowpane was cold to my touch, signaling the approach of winter. You could smell the remnants of last evening's fire in our hearth.

A huge maple tree on our lawn caught my eye. I watched in wonder as a leaf—the color of a golden sunset—drifted slowly from the safety of its branch. At first I felt sad. For as lovely as the leaf was, the very brilliance of its hue signaled its death.

I watched in amazement as the leaf was softly scooped up by the wind and gently tossed in the air, drifting up and down and away as it played its own unique game with nature. It was then I realized that the leaf falling from the tree to its death was more fully alive than I was. At least the leaf was participating in a spontaneous adventure with the wind, with no restrictions on time or fear of its ultimate destination. The leaf was fully present in the moment. It was I, who caught up in my expected roles, seemed to be withering.

Life, I had come to believe, was a series of scripted dramas. Some dramas are painful, others merely annoying. Each of us plays a certain role depending upon our circumstances. Lately it seemed as if the dramas never ended. Once one script came to its merciful end, another took its place.

Sometimes my daughter took center stage, requiring my time and attention. Often it was my husband. Rarely did I assume center stage. These days I seemed to play a supporting role in everyone else's scripted drama. Life had become a blur of merging sagas.

Once again the falling leaves caught my eye. The leaves were not acting out scripts. Their movements were neither expected nor robotic. Caught up with the wind, theirs was a dance not a drama. For a time I lost myself in the beauty of their dance.

My husband came home a short time later looking especially tired and wan. His round jovial face was etched with furrowed lines. He looked weary and much older than his fifty-one years. His eyes, normally so mischievous and blue, seemed dull, devoid of any sparkle. He didn't say much, but his entire demeanor seemed one of defeat.

"Let's go for a ride, Susan," he said.

"Where?" I asked, annoyed. After all, I had dinner cooking on the stove and my daughter was due home soon.

"You'll see," was his only reply.

Grabbing my hand, I had little choice but to follow. I paused at the doorway and instinctively reached behind me fumbling for my invisible knapsack. I couldn't leave home without it. I carried it everywhere. It was filled with my baggage, all those unresolved issues from the past. Finding it right where it belonged, strapped to my back, I nodded, ready to proceed. I glanced at my husband. I could tell by the stoop of his shoulders that his knapsack of baggage was fixed in place as well. We never spoke about it, but every day our invisible backpacks seemed heavier and more burdensome to carry.

Shortly I found myself at a deserted airfield. It was more like a dirt runway with no other planes in sight.

"What are we doing here?"

Again he responded, "You'll see."

In the distance, I saw an airplane, if you could call it that. It was a tiny two-seater, propeller-driven contraption made of tin. "What's that?"

My husband turned and looked at me with a gaze of total bewilderment. "It's my latest possession," he said. "Let's go for a ride."

I looked at him in disbelief. This strange machine looked more like a sculptured piece of metal rather than a functional plane.

"You must be kidding!" I chided. "This is a toy, not a plane."

"No!" he retorted angrily. "It's my tin plane. No one else has one like it."

My husband is no small fellow. Standing 6'3" tall and weighing 250 lb., it took great effort to hoist himself up into the small tin plane. He turned and offered me his hand. Still thinking it was a joke, I allowed him to lift me into the tiny cockpit.

"Are we going to pretend to fly?" I said sarcastically.

"No," he responded firmly. "This is my plane, and I will fly it."

With that, he started the engine of the little tin plane. The contraption made a ferocious noise as he gunned the motor. It shook violently as we started down the dirt runway. Terrified, I froze in my seat as he nudged the joystick forward and the tin plane slowly rose off the ground.

With his gaze fixed firmly ahead, my husband steered the plane as it struggled to rise in the air. It couldn't climb very high, just high enough to clear the treetops.

Trembling, I dared to ask, "Where are we going?"

He turned to me but didn't smile. "We're going to see our possessions. I want to see what I own. I want to see if it's worth it."

It was not just his words that disturbed me. It was his entire demeanor. "To see if what's worth it?"

"The struggle," he replied. "The horrible day in, day out struggle."

Within moments our little world came into focus. I looked down and saw our white brick, two-story home, our pets, and even my daughter. The garage door was open. Inside I saw our new red corvette. We had purchased the car for my husband—sort of a midlife crisis thing. The car represented a temporary diversion and one more expensive payment.

As storm clouds gathered in the distance, I studied our world. Everything appeared to be in order, and yet I felt an incredible void. I was reminded of a merry-go-round with no beginning and no end. By the standard of the day, I had everything a woman could desire—a loving husband, a terrific daughter, a fine home. I had more possessions than I could hope to care for, and more responsibility than I could bear.

I tried to buoy my spirits. My sadness made no sense. My life was, if not completely fulfilling, at least manageable. I tried to assume my expected roles with a measure of grace and aplomb. I thought it was my responsibility to keep the family intact, with uplifted spirits and objectives clearly in sight. If nothing else, while I often loathed my supporting role, at least I felt needed. I was the glue that held the family together ... or so I thought.

My husband had turned to face me. He circled the tin plane slowly overhead our well-ordered life and our many possessions.

"I have something to tell you," he cried above the engine's roar.

There was something about the tone of his voice that frightened me.

"I lost everything today ... my job ... our health insurance ... and all our security."

His words were a faraway echo in my ears. They made no sense. I felt an overwhelming sense of fear, but I didn't have time to focus. For just then, as he found the strength to tell me what secret he harbored, the plane began shaking violently, whirling around and around before spinning totally out of control. The plane—our lives—crashed in that moment into a raging sea of darkness and despair.

Suddenly the plane and my husband had vanished. I was alone in raging waters battling for my life. I had never experienced total terror before, until now. I fought with all my might to prevent sheer panic from paralyzing me as I tried desperately to stay afloat. I had to retain my ability to think and reason. I couldn't succumb to desperation. I pummeled the waves, gasping for air. The struggle was futile. Sinking under for the third time, I realized that I was drowning. The highlights of my life flashed before me. Inwardly I screamed that it wasn't enough. There was so much more I hoped to accomplish. I had the sense of a mission I'd left undone.

From somewhere deep within the core of my being, I mustered my last remaining energy and with all my heart and soul cried out: "GOD HELP ME!"

I shut my eyes, preparing to die. A bright light, with the speed and accuracy of a laser beam, parted the water. I was engulfed in the light. Gently but with great power, I was lifted from the bottom of the ocean—the darkness—into the light. Then the beam of light evaporated, and I found myself alone again on the surface of the water, struggling to stay afloat.

Gasping for air, I searched for my husband. I couldn't find him. Feeling more fear than I had in my entire lifetime, I screamed in terror.

A fog had settled over the water, but in the distance I saw a man standing in a small boat. The sea was choppy, stinging my eyes with salt water and causing the small vessel to rock back and forth in the waves. I couldn't see the man's face clearly.

"My husband is missing!" I shouted. "I think he's drowned!"

Gulping water, I struggled to stay afloat.

I cried out, "PLEASE, IN THE NAME OF GOD, HELP ME!"

I expected the man to react with the same urgency that I felt. Instead, he remained calm and merely smiled as he maneuvered his worn vessel toward me. His features slowly sharpened. He had a strong, handsome face weathered by the salty air. His smile seemed kind.

"Don't be afraid. I can help you," he said with a voice that was reassuring and calm. "The choice, however, is entirely yours."

As I furiously treaded water trying desperately to stay afloat, I thought the man to be a lunatic. Of course I wanted to be rescued. Who wouldn't?

Wave by wave, the boat came closer.

"Are you certain you want my help? It means accepting the ride all the way."

I couldn't find the right words to express my confusion. Here I was drowning in a black raging sea. This man was the only person in sight who could save me. What choice did I have but to accept his help? Perhaps the man had been lost at sea too long himself. He seemed deranged.

Yet I felt a stirring inside, that there might be a measure of truth to his words. I did have a choice. I could succumb to my own despair and drown, or I could fight to live. To what end? I didn't dare fathom.

I realized that succumbing to despair might be the easier solution. Yet in that critical moment, I chose life over death.

"SAVE ME!"

The stranger threw me a rope. With amazing strength, he pulled me to the bow of his small craft, then lifted me aboard. I was trembling from the cold and fright. He grabbed a blanket and threw it around my shoulders. Then he embraced me. His touch felt like a surge of electricity racing through my body. Instantly, I felt warm.

Leading me to the stern, he sat down opposite me. I felt safe in his gentle presence. I started to express my gratitude, but I didn't even know his name.

"Who are you?" I asked

"Does it matter?" he said.

"Yes, it matters very much. Please tell me your name."

"You may call me whatever you like."

Other than my daughter, I'd never had the opportunity to name someone. I wasn't sure what to do. I carefully studied the man's face. His features were strong, as if they'd been chiseled. His deep-set eyes were an intriguing mixture of turquoise and teal, like an ocean on a bright summer day. He appeared to be a fisherman, a man of the sea, yet I felt honored to be in his presence.

I'm not sure why, but a courageous name came to me. It seemed to fit the man seated before me.

"I shall call you Christopher. But please tell me, who are you? How did you know I needed your help?"

His answer was simple. "I am one of your many guides. I've always been here to help you. All you had to do was ask."

I had heard of spirit guides before, but I'd never met one face to face. Before I could introduce myself, he read my mind like the pages of an open book.

"You'd be surprised, Susan, how many people would rather drown in despair than call out to the Source of hope and safety. Look around you."

Following his direction, I gazed out into the endless sea. It was a shock to realize that we had not crashed alone into the sea of despair. At the time, I could neither see nor hear anyone else. Yet the murky waters were filled with desperate souls, each in various stages of drowning. Suddenly I thought about my husband and I started to panic. Tears filled my eyes.

"We have to find my husband."

Christopher's voice was not unkind, yet his response was firm.

"Every human being has to make his own choice. You cannot make it for him. Help is always present if only you choose to see. But each person must ask in their own way."

Christopher leaned forward and wiped away my tears. "You cried out for help and your prayer was answered. There's no place where you are that God isn't. There's nowhere in the universe where you begin and God ends. Yet man would rather perish than realize and acknowledge this simple truth."

I couldn't stop crying. I wanted to find my husband. I couldn't bear the thought of losing him now.

Christopher's smile warmed me. "Your husband must make his pilgrimage without you. His guide is with him as I'm here for you. We have many people to walk with us through the journey of life, yet each person must seek his own answers and walk the path in single file. You can reach out and take the hand of another, but ultimately you must fulfill your purpose for being ... alone."

He bade me glance at all the desperate souls once again. "What do you see?"

My eyes searched the sea. I saw a few. people like me reaching out for a power greater than themselves. Instantly they, too, found themselves in the safety of a life raft. But there were many others flailing their arms about in a futile attempt to master their demons. As I gazed out into treacherous waters with no hint of a shoreline in sight, I wondered how they'd ever make it to safety.

Christopher answered the thought for me.

"They won't. Most of them will drown in their own despair. There is only one sure way to find your destiny. That's here and now with me."

Christopher glanced away for a moment. When he returned his gaze to me, there was no hint of laughter in his eyes.

"I must warn you that the journey will not be easy. It never is. Do you understand?"

I didn't understand at all. Living life was hard enough. I couldn't imagine a journey that would be more difficult than the life I had been leading, acting out endless dramas, one saga merging into another. Instinctively I reached back, searching for my knapsack. I thought it to be the essence of what defined me. It was still in place. I'd not lost my sense of self in the murky waters.

"You may choose to release your baggage at any time, Susan. Ultimately that is the goal of your journey home. You can do it now or as you feel comfortable in small segments along the way. The choice is always yours."

There was a part of me that yearned to throw my baggage overboard. Yet I clung to my past hurts and disappointments. My story, with all the triumphs and the tragedies, defined me. My particular backpack of memories distinguished me from all others. I was afraid to surrender what I believed to be the essence of myself. For a little longer, I chose to keep my baggage secured in place.

*T*ime had no relevance in the sea of despair. The present moment merely evolved into another present moment. Time—which I could not measure without a watch—merely passed until darkness descended all around.

Exhaustion consumed me. I tried to ignore the fatigue because I wanted to stay awake. I felt it imperative to make sure that Christopher, with strong, steady hands, steered the boat straight ahead. I didn't see the absurdity of my thoughts. I didn't even know where I was, much less where we were heading. It was Christopher who knew the way, Christopher who guided the boat, Christopher who had rescued me from drowning. What arrogance to think I needed to direct my savior. Finally, shaking my head in gloom, I realized that there was absolutely nothing I could do by myself to alter my fate.

I re-wrapped the blanket securely about me. The constant rocking of the boat was a gentle lullaby inviting me to sleep. I awoke with the first rays of dawn. As I opened my eyes, I wondered if my nightmare might only be a dream from which I could awaken.

I glanced around hopefully, but nothing had changed. I was still in a life raft, seemingly adrift in the sea of despair. The man I chose to call Christopher was still at the helm. I was surrounded by black water stretching as far as my eyes could see with no beginning and no end.

"Where are we going?" I whispered despondently.

Christopher turned and greeted me warmly. "Ah, you're awake, Susan. I hope you rested well."

He stood and stretched. I wondered if he'd been sitting in the captain's chair all night. He came toward me holding out two steaming mugs of freshly brewed coffee. I gazed at him quizzically. How in the name of God could he brew a cup of coffee in a rowboat at sea?

"I know you like coffee first thing in the morning."

"But how?"

Christopher's mouth curled with amusement, but he didn't answer. Instead, he chose a seat opposite mine and sipped his own mug of coffee thoughtfully.

I dared to repeat my earlier question. "Where are we going?"

His smile was warm and confident, but his words made no sense. "We're going wherever the journey takes us."

A feeling of misery consumed me. Here I was in the middle of a raging sea with a man who spoke in riddles. I couldn't find my husband, and my daughter didn't even realize I was missing. Didn't he comprehend my terror? Didn't he understand how desperately I wanted to go home? What I didn't know was that Christopher understood in ways far beyond my mortal comprehension.

Savoring the unusually rich flavor of the coffee, I quietly observed Christopher. He was a humble, unassuming man, yet his presence was a commanding one, inspiring confidence and trust. I found myself mesmerized by his eyes. His eyes reflected deep wisdom. Just who was this man and why was he here?

"Why has this happened?" I asked.

Once again, his response made no sense. "It happened because it had to."

Christopher leaned back against the cushions of his seat. Then he cast his eyes to the sea.

"Think about your life, Susan, at the precise moment you left it. Remember what was happening. Recall what you were feeling."

My mind returned to the scene outside the huge picture window in my living room. Once again I saw the majestic maple tree on our lawn and recalled the gentle descent of the falling leaf. For some strange reason, with the remembrance of the leaf, tears came to my eyes.

"What is your sadness about?" Christopher asked.

A tear ran down my cheek as I thought about the leaf that was experiencing more joy in death than I was in living.

"I've spent my entire life doing what I thought was expected. I have everything I ever wanted, but no matter what I have or what I get, it never seems enough."

"Keep digging," Christopher urged. "Tell me more."

"From the time I was five years old, I wanted to do something really special with my life. I wanted to make a difference. I had a vision. Throughout my life, I permitted other people to deter me. I listened to the voices of all those who said I couldn't achieve my dreams because they were too risky. So, instead of pursuing my dreams, I followed the norm. I married, divorced, raised a child, married again. I worked very hard to create a world where we could feel comfortable and secure. I reasoned that someday when the needs of my family were finally met, it would be time to realize my own dream."

I cast my eyes into the sea of despair. "No matter how hard I've tried to be ordinary, I never felt like I quite fit in."

"Of course you didn't fit in," Christopher responded gently. "How could you? Spirit is God's boundless energy yearning for expression. God's sweet Spirit, which is the essence of you, yearns to dance with all creation, expressing Itself as you. But you have no idea who you are or how to do it, so you waste your precious days with frenzied activity or robotic routines. Your spirit, your God Self, remains trapped within the confines of your human body. Yet in every moment and with every breath of precious life, your spirit yearns to break free to dance with the angels. Of course you don't fit in. Your spirit was never meant to."

Rising, Christopher went to the helm of the boat and turned the wheel sharply to the right, correcting course. When he was satisfied, he returned to the seat near me.

"You asked why this happened? Let me respond. You sensed a tremendous void in your life because you were not fulfilling your Divine Destiny. You were wasting your energy trying to create a world that felt safe and secure. You were merely acting out your life—scripted dramas of your own creation—not living it. From the depths of your being you cried out for purpose and direction. Well, your prayers have been answered. But then ... in one form or fashion ... they always are."

I stared at my rescuer aghast. Surely he was not suggesting that I had prayed to be cast adrift at sea with a stranger who made no sense. Well, if that be so, God has a twisted sense of humor. It was time for the cosmic joke to end.

"I want to go home now."

Christopher's response startled me. "Home is exactly where we're heading. But home is not quite where you think."

Christopher remained silent for a time, leaving me alone to ponder. It was true that I had worked exceedingly hard just to be ordinary. I had the kind of existence that other people admired, yet I didn't feel truly alive. What went wrong, I asked myself.

Christopher answered my question.

"You created an existence based on your own fuel—power and control, the essence of which is fear. Sooner or later your fuel runs out. The security you erroneously think you have attained becomes, like a tin plane, vulnerable to the turbulent winds of life. Then your world crashes, and you plunge into your sea of despair. Of and by yourself, this is the only existence you are capable of creating."

Christopher took my hand and cradled it warmly. "But there's more to life, Susan. So much more."

I felt reassured by his touch. It felt safe to continue.

"What do you mean that I created an existence based on my own fuel of power and control?"

"Let me show you," he said.

Christopher offered me a seat next to his at the helm. Focusing straight ahead, he piloted the vessel. All I could see for miles in any direction was an endless sea of water. Then suddenly out of nowhere an island appeared.

"Land!" I cried. "I see land!"

Christopher directed our boat toward land. Within seconds we found ourselves at the shore of a small island. Christopher slowed the boat. I could reach out and nearly touch the green grass.

Pointing to the center of the island, Christopher said, "Look over there. What do you see?"

My eyes followed where he pointed, and I saw vegetation laden with mangos, pineapple, guava and coconuts. There was luscious green grass all around. In the center of the island, I made out the shape of a figure. I wanted to cry out at seeing another human being. I peered closer and saw it was a dark-haired woman. She seemed strangely familiar as she slowly turned to face us. She wasn't a young woman. I guessed her to be about forty. I wanted desperately to know who she was and why she was here.

When our eyes finally met, I gasped. I struggled to remain calm and focused. For there standing before me ... was my mirror image. But she couldn't be me. I was here. She was there in the center of an island clad in a garment made of mud and leaves. In her right hand, she held a coconut. Directly behind her was a shelter made out of twigs and branches. I ... she ... seemed healthy enough. There was a pleasant golden cast to her face and arms. She seemed content, although it was obvious that she was very much alone on this island.

I was awed at the woman's ability to survive. She was all alone, and yet she somehow managed to clothe and feed herself and construct a shelter.

"What is this about?" I asked Christopher.

Before he could answer, we heard the roar of wind. Storm clouds appeared directly over the center of the island. The wind began lashing about. The woman had no time to flee. There she stood in the center of the island, totally unprotected, at the mercy of the furious storm. The wind tore the clothes from her body as the rain pelted her with the ferocity of piercing shards of glass. The shelter she had constructed was blown away in a rush of wind. The rain fell so fast and hard that the fruit fell from the trees, spoiling instantly as it splattered in a heap on the ground.

In the span of only a few minutes, her very survival was jeopardized. The meager necessities she'd taken for granted were destroyed. From the safety of the boat, I felt terrible fear and sorrow. How would she survive? How would I have survived?

"That's a pretty ghastly sight, isn't it?" Christopher asked.

"It's horrible," I replied. "What are you trying to show me?"

"The picture you see here is not that different from the existence you created for yourself. This island represents the life you have chosen. This is true for most people here on earth at this time. By your own wits, you find the means for your basic

survival. The quality of existence is not much different whether the struggle is on a remote island or in a thriving city. You languish in jobs you detest, thinking you must in order to purchase your shelter, clothe your bodies and buy your processed food. For a time you survive with your basic needs met and your lives routinely paced. You feel a great emptiness, but delude yourselves into thinking you are safe and in control. You live in fear. You fear to live.

"You trade the joyous adventure of life for the deathtrap you call security. Fueled only by human power, rather than Spirit's power, you are just as vulnerable to the unpredictable storms of life as you are on the island."

Just as quickly as it had appeared, the island vanished.

"What happens then?"

"You either choose in that moment to drown in the sea of despair or you cry out for God's help. Sound familiar?"

I nodded.

Christopher's gentle eyes held me. "I'd like to see you end the cycle and begin the journey home."

We traveled on for a short while in silence. While he focused straight ahead, piloting the boat, I scrutinized him carefully. It was as if I'd known him all my life. I felt safe and secure in his presence. There was something about him ... his smell, his touch, his aura, that seemed as familiar as my own face in the mirror. This was not someone I had just met.

"I was wondering how long it would take," said he.

"For what?"

"Until you remembered."

"You've been with me a long time, haven't you?"

"I've been your guide ever since you were a tiny girl. We used to play when you were a child. Your parents teased you about your invisible friend because you could see me."

"You looked different then."

"When you were a child, I looked like a child in spirit form. To fit your need for a rescuer at sea, I took on this form. What difference does it make what you or we look like? The essence of you never changes. Some people see their guides as angels, others as animals or other beings."

"What does a guide do?"

"Your guides are your teachers and best friends if only you will allow them to be. We have no other purpose than to help and direct you. It is our sacred mission. I have been sent by God to guide you through the experiences of this lifetime. Through this service, my soul evolves."

"Are you always by my side?"

"Always," Christopher replied. "Remember when you were five months pregnant and it was Christmas? You were spending the holiday with your mother. Your father had recently died. You presumed the child you were carrying was a boy. You wanted to name your son after your father."

"Yes! I wanted to name the baby Joseph Daniel. I planned to call him Joey."

"What happened?" Christopher asked.

"I was walking through the garage to my mother's apartment when I suddenly heard a quiet voice whispering to think again about a name because the child I was carrying was a girl not a boy."

Christopher smiled. "That was me. Do you remember the time you were supposed to attend the tea dance?"

"Yes, the Friday night tea dance at the Hyatt Hotel. I'd been there the two Fridays before, standing in my favorite spot underneath the skywalk to listen to the band. I was anxious to go again. I'd made plans to join friends there at six o'clock. At the last minute, I received a dinner invitation from someone I really wanted to see. I felt an overwhelming urge to forgo the dance and go to the dinner instead."

A chill ran through me.

"I would have been there, standing under the skywalk when it collapsed if it had not been for that unexpected dinner invitation. Seeing that particular person that night was the only thing more important than the dance."

Christopher's eyes sparkled when he spoke. "I arranged that meeting to keep you from harm. We can help you in anything from the mundane to the critical if only you ask. Sometimes—like that night—we are permitted to intervene to keep you from harm or from participating in something to which your soul has not agreed. But usually you must ask for our help. We can't interfere with your free will, but if you still your mind and ask, you can discern our guidance."

"How can I be sure that what I hear is coming from my guides?"

"Guidance begins as a gentle whisper or feeling. Sometimes it can turn into a gnawing in the stomach, signaling that something isn't quite right. Sometimes when I want you to pay attention, you feel my nudge."

I knew exactly what Christopher meant. "I have felt your touch on my left shoulder like a soft vibration."

"As your awareness of our presence grows, we are able to fine-tune our communication. The more you recognize the connection and open the channel, the more easily we can communicate with you until it becomes second nature. We speak in symbols, dreams, words or simply knowingness. We develop a language all our own. Oftentimes when you quiet the mind, particularly in meditation, our guidance comes in the form of thoughts. They are not random thoughts of the mental mind. They are whisperings from the heart. Our words may sound like yours, but the essence is very different from your frantic or mundane mental activity. Our words speak to your heart and soul."

"What's the difference between my guardian angel and you?" I humbly inquired.

"An angel is a direct messenger to and from God. Your prayers float on an angel's wings straight to the Creator. But before we talk about angels, let's discuss the concept of God. You must understand that God is neither male nor female. God is not a person or a thing. God simply IS. God is the totality of everything. You may picture God as you like or call the Creator whatever name you wish. For purposes of our discussion and because this is the terminology commonly used, we will refer to God as He, but don't limit your experience of God to a paternal figure residing on a throne in the sky.

"Now back to the subject of angels," Christopher continued. "Everyone is assigned a guardian angel at birth, usually for protection. Your guardian angel remains by your side throughout life and the process you call death, which is nothing more than a transition into another dimension. Life is eternal and everlasting.

"Your guide is more like a kindred spirit, a best friend, a teacher. You have many different guides throughout your lifetime, depending upon your needs and level of understanding. I am your primary guide. I've been with you the longest. I will be with you until you have no further need of me and my assignment is finished. You will always have the guides you need to fulfill your Divine Destiny. All you have to do is ask for the assistance you require—from the mundane to the complicated."

"How does that work? How are you able to know what is best for me?"

"We have understanding from a broader viewpoint. We know the blueprint your soul has chosen this lifetime. We know what you have agreed to accomplish or to experience for your soul's evolution. We know the easiest way to direct you. We have perspective."

"Perspective?"

"Each person views life from his own seat overlooking the huge arena of experiences. Your seat on the ledge is your perspective.

Unless you become one with another, you can't possibly understand anyone else's experiences or perceptions. That's why you have no right to judge the actions of another. How can you know what is in another's heart or what they've come to earth to learn? That's why bigotry and prejudice are so terribly wrong."

Christopher gazed for a moment out to sea, as if measuring his words, before continuing.

"Each person knows and represents certain truths. This knowledge arises out of the experiences of all your past lifetimes. You carry within yourself a lovely little piece of a huge, grand Mosaic. Because your piece is profound, you erroneously believe it is complete. Your piece is exquisite, but it's only the tiniest fragment of an infinite whole.

"You—mankind—think your truth is ultimate Truth. Certain religions or religious movements claim to have sole knowledge of God, the one true doctrine, the only way. How arrogant! How ignorant! How can man begin to comprehend the vastness of that which you call God? Our truths are only the perspectives we are capable of understanding at the present time. Your understanding of Truth, or God, expands as you gain wisdom and knowledge. No one has ever glimpsed the infinite Mosaic. It takes each person bringing his own piece—sharing his concept of God and truth—to create the whole picture. That's why every human being is precious."

Christopher leaned forward and said, "In order for you to realize your piece of the grand Mosaic, you have to make the journey home."

It was then I finally understood that home was not the house I'd left behind.

*I*n order to journey home, you must leave the chaos you've created behind."

"How do I do that?" I asked. "Where do I begin?"

"You begin right where you are," he replied.

"Here?" I countered.

"Anywhere you find yourself is exactly the place to begin. Close your eyes."

Ready beyond measure to begin my journey home, I closed my eyes. I had no idea where we were going, but I realized one thing. Anywhere we traveled would be better than here, lost in the sea of despair.

"Quiet yourself, Susan. Become centered and focused. Release any tension you are holding. Feel the gentle rocking of the boat. Breathe. Surrender to the moment and to the experience."

As I turned within, Christopher's voice faded. "You take breathing for granted," he said. "Yet every breath you take is a gift of life."

An amazing awareness filled my mind. How many times in an hour, a day, in a year, do we draw a precious breath never realizing what we're doing? Never comprehending that without this simple process, life as we know it here would cease to exist. Breathing is the ultimate gift of life.

"Allow your lungs to fill, then hold your breath for a few seconds, giving thanks to Spirit for the precious gift of life."

I obeyed, first filling my lungs and then slowly exhaling, only to repeat the process again. Quickly I found myself relaxing. Focusing only upon my breath and the gentle rocking of the boat, I lost my awareness of the sea. Letting go of my fear, I immediately felt peace.

"Now gently allow Spirit to enter your consciousness. Visualize a spiritual symbol, something or someone that holds special meaning for you."

At first I saw the face of Jesus. His gentle eyes were filled with compassion. His face was kind, his smile reassuring. He nodded as if he approved of my experience. My eyes were then drawn to his heart, the sacred heart of Jesus, which he cradled in his hand. It was a brilliant-red, beating heart filled with immense love and compassion.

I became absorbed in his being. Feeling indescribable joy, I watched the image of Jesus depart as another came into focus. It was the lovely face of a young woman. She had delicate skin and exquisite sapphire-blue eyes. Long raven curls framed her face. I asked her name.

"My name is Melanie Grace. I'm your guardian angel."

I was captivated by the protective yet peaceful presence of my guardian angel as she hovered above a tranquil scene that slowly

appeared. The raging water was replaced by a crystal-clear lake of sky blue. I was no longer in Christopher's boat but in a long, slender gondola. Seated in the rear of the gondola, I was wearing a long, flowered skirt made of gauze, spread neatly about my ankles. I wore a high-neck, white satin blouse. A large straw hat rested by my side. A small book lay open upon my lap.

For a moment I couldn't see who was steering the gondola. At first it didn't matter because I was quite content to find myself exactly where I was. But slowly, a large man with a familiar presence turned to face me. It was my husband. He showed no sign of recognition. After a brief glance, he returned his attention to the gondola and the water. Yet, as if frozen in time, the gondola did not move; nothing stirred.

My awareness shifted to the scene around me. While Melanie Grace hovered just above, to my right was a white swan. Its slender neck curved gracefully as it floated with poise. To its right was a black duckling. Unlike the swan, the duckling's feathers were short and frayed. Yet I found both creatures captivating. Their eyes beheld one another with wonder.

Just beyond the duckling was a frog seated comfortably upon a lily pad. I could smell the sweet fragrance of lilies. I could hear the frog's resonant croaking.

I heard myself asking Melanie Grace what the splendid scene represented.

It was Christopher who responded. "Soon enough you'll have your answer, Susan. It's the purpose of journeying home."

I didn't want the images to fade. I felt great peace drifting upon the placid lake with my husband piloting the slender vessel, my angel standing guard, and the swan, duckling and frog by my side.

We came to a waterfall. Suddenly, I found myself spiraling down the waterfall in the gondola. I came to a stop, landing feet first at the entrance of a glistening cave.

*F*or the first time since climbing on board the tin plane and crashing into the sea of despair, I stood on firm ground. The lake, with its gondola and creatures, had vanished. I felt alone and afraid.

Christopher suddenly materialized. "You are never alone."

He seemed sad. "You have been given the gift of free will, which can serve or destroy you. It is your choice whether to dwell in fear or to move through it. You cannot move forward in fear. Love is your natural state of being. Fear is what you create to justify separating from God."

The cave was no ordinary cave. Rather than being constructed of rock, it was made of pure, glistening gold. I marveled at the sight.

"It is through this cave that you enter the Kingdom of Heaven where eternal life resides. Herein lies the seat of knowledge and wisdom. Inside are the answers to all your questions."

I stood in awe. "Where am I?" I asked.

With reverence, Christopher said, "You are standing before the golden, jeweled cave of yourself."

"The golden, jeweled cave of myself?"

"Your soul."

A force within the cave beckoned me to enter. I froze, not knowing what to do, yet I felt a tremendous pull.

"Your soul contains the jewels of wisdom acquired over lifetimes. In order to understand why you plunged into the sea of despair, you must go within to find your truth."

"Will you come with me?" I asked.

"No," Christopher replied firmly. "The first steps of the journey home are yours to take alone, but Spirit is all around you, in and through you, guiding you every moment."

I took a tentative step forward. Christopher stopped me.

"Your soul is a consecrated place. To enter the holy temple of your soul, you must leave your baggage behind. The true essence of you is too sacred to be littered with negativity. If you will surrender your baggage to me, I will see that it is safely guarded and respected. It will be returned to you in due time ... if you desire."

I'd almost forgotten the knapsack I carried with me. Waking, sleeping, I kept it close always. Whenever I chose to feel sad, I could reach into the past and wallow in my failures. I was reluctant to release my baggage now. Somehow it had served me, justifying my shortcomings in the present because of patterns ingrained in the past. But the mysteries contained within the cave were more enticing. I surrendered the knapsack.

"Melanie Grace will stand guard at the entrance of your soul. You are to go within and explore as much of yourself as you wish. Take your time and go slowly. You have all of eternity to complete the journey. Experience yourself with patience using all your senses. There are many jewels contained within your being. You have not arrived at this point by accident. You have much to accomplish. But there are things about yourself and your purpose that you need to know in order to achieve mastery. You may select three gems of wisdom to guide you."

Christopher's eyes held mine. "You cannot make a mistake. You will be divinely led. God knows what you need. God cherishes your heart's desires and wants you to experience the joyful life envisioned when He created you. Think about your own daughter. Haven't you always desired only her highest good—that which would bring her joy, fulfillment and happiness? Do you think your Creator wants any less for you?"

"When will I see you again?" I asked.

"After your selection, I will meet you in the Crystal Chamber of Illumination. There the mystery of the gems you have selected will be revealed. So venture inward, Susan. Most precious gifts await."

I felt a tremendous urge to enter the cave, but suddenly I grew frightened. What if I became lost? What if I couldn't find my way back to the existence I knew here? My eyes sought Christopher's.

"You are attached to the earth plane by an invisible cord. When you are ready, you will be allowed to return to the existence you have known and chosen for yourself. Fear not. You walk your path individually, but you never walk alone."

With tentative feet, I stepped inside the golden jeweled cave of myself. I expected the cave to be like a structure on the physical plane, formidable and dark. Instead, the golden jeweled cave of my soul was like an opulent, mythical temple. I had been told that I would make the journey alone, yet I felt a Presence, omnipotent and all-knowing. A blanket of golden light illuminated my path. The floor was like a velvet carpet beneath my feet.

As I journeyed within, the gentle melody of a violin surrounded me. It was a lovely, sweet sound that I felt more than heard. My body, mind and spirit harmonized with its vibrations. I could smell the fragrance of lilies, leaving a sweet taste in my mouth.

The cave did not spiral downward so much as extend beyond what I would have thought to be the physical limitations of space and time. In the far distance I could see the misty haze of a bright, white light. I wondered if that was the tunnel to heaven.

I stood still and glanced in all directions as far as I could see. There were gems everywhere. Each jewel was magnificent, one more beautiful than the next. Some were clearly visible, suspended in air, while others adorned the walls of the cave. A precious few were more obscured, seemingly in areas just beyond my grasp.

I had never seen such pure gems. The colors were extraordinary. Coming from the physical plane, I couldn't begin to describe the colors that I saw—blues, pinks and golden indigo. Sapphires blended with diamonds, emeralds with rubies and opals with garnets. But the colors were fluid, changing form with my different perspective. I wondered how in the midst of such splendor, I would know which gems to choose.

I heard Christopher's soft voice saying, "All the jewels are yours, Susan, like the wisdom and knowledge of self, yours for the choosing. Feel your way. You will know what is yours to select in the moment. Go deep within yourself, down and through the cave, as you feel led. Remember, you are attached to the cord of life, the cord of eternity. You cannot fall or lose your way. You are one with and a part of all creation."

Having no sense of time, I explored the cave as thoroughly as I dared. Secured by the cord of attachment, I journeyed deeper within myself. The farther I went, the more clearly I saw the pathway to heaven illuminated by a beacon of white light. I felt a great magnetic pull toward the light. I sensed, with every step I took, great peace and understanding.

Glimpses of my life flashed before me, projects I'd left undone, like the pages of my novel locked away in a desk drawer. People I knew and loved came into my awareness, especially my daughter.

"How could I leave her behind?" I thought.

I felt a sudden jar as the cord by which I was attached tightened, pulling me back from the light that beckoned. The pain and emptiness of living seemed overwhelming. Every day on earth had become a struggle, devoid of joy, to survive. I wanted more than anything to run toward the light, to escape earth and to embrace heaven.

Yet there was a force inside me that willed me to stop. My life's work had not been completed. I wasn't even sure of my purpose. To exit now would leave too many tasks undone. I turned away from the light and focused upon exploring that which felt safe. I didn't dare look back to the pathway to heaven. I remained where I could see the entrance to the cave from where I'd come.

Feeling a rush of cool wind on my right cheek, I turned abruptly. There hidden in a crevice was an incredible jewel, different from the rest. The brilliance of the gem enticed me. I moved closer for a better look. This jewel seemed more difficult to reach than the others did. The path became a maze with obstacles to overcome. Yet the splendid jewel beckoned.

There was a quivering sensation in the center of my forehead as I reached for the precious jewel. The heat that radiated from the gem caused my hand to tingle. I hesitated just inches away as a wave of energy surged through me. I knew then, without a doubt, that this was the sacred jewel intended for my selection.

My hand trembled as I reached for the jewel. It was not attached to the wall, but I could not remove it easily. Finally, after carefully grasping and rotating it, I felt it fall into my hand. I held it tightly. The jewel was the size of a grapefruit. There was something odd about what I thought to be only the first of three jewels I was to choose. As I brought the gem closer, I was stunned to see that there was not one distinct jewel but three entwined within what appeared to be a multifaceted diamond. There was a circular ruby, a triangular emerald, and a sapphire in the form of a figure-eight design. Ribbons of color flowed in and around the three gems—magnificent hues of lavender, turquoise and gold.

I felt a tremendous surge of energy as I touched the gem. I realized then that whatever I was to learn had three distinct qualities melded together for a higher purpose. I knew without a doubt that this was the jewel—the blessing—for which I had made the journey home.

*M*y hand trembled as I held the jewel. I wondered what I should do. Then I heard Christopher's voice whispering, "You have chosen well, Susan. Follow my voice to the Chamber of Illumination where the first of your answers await."

I felt a thrilling tingle as I followed my instincts down a narrow corridor to the right. The jewel vibrated in my hand while the fluid colors danced to their own music, shimmering with different colored lights and hues with every step I took.

Suddenly a magnificent chamber appeared before me. There was a cool, blue light radiating from it. It was similar to the light that marked the pathway to heaven.

This room was different from the cave. The walls and ceiling of the chamber were constructed of crystals. Rainbow colored lights twinkled from the crystals. I felt honored to be allowed into such a hallowed place. The Chamber of Illumination, unlike the cave, was cool with blue bright light radiating everywhere. I glanced above. Through the crystal ceiling I glimpsed the moon and the stars. I felt the wisdom of eternity.

I closed my eyes and gave thanks for the Presence that I felt. When I opened my eyes, I saw Christopher. We were not alone. The chamber was filled with spirits, each with a distinct shape and persona. The spirits looked human, only their bodies were lighter and more transparent. But their features were clearly discernible. I was surprised, yet at ease, with the group that had assembled. I started to ask Christopher who they were. He answered before I could speak.

"Throughout one's life, many guides and teachers come to assist with every stage of growth, and every need, perceived or not. All your guides have assembled for this wondrous moment. Our work is greatly rewarded when the one we are assigned to help seeks answers from deep within. We work an entire lifetime to

bring you to this point. We are honored to be with you now. Every time you go within and select a precious gem of yourself to know and understand, you make the journey home for all of us that much easier."

I smiled and with great wonder gazed at my guides one at a time. I saw faces that I recognized. One was my father, another my grandmother. I realized Christopher's words were true. My father and my grandmother were no longer present on the earth plane, but their love and our bond were as strong as ever.

Christopher said, "Our dear ones never leave us. Even though we can no longer see or touch them, we can call upon them anytime we wish. And they come."

My guides, in spirit form, were as alive and tangible as any loved one still in the physical body. I realized then that death is nothing but a transition from one dimension to the next. In death, we shed the earthly vehicle we no longer need, but we never lose those we love. They are always with us, lifetime through lifetime. We are eternally one.

There were many spirits whom I did not recognize, yet I felt the same bond and connection. One was an old Indian woman, the other a Frenchman. There was a young girl who resembled me. I knew her to be the aunt for whom I'd been named but never met. She had died at sixteen of an illness long before I was born. I wanted to embrace all of them. I bowed to them with respect and love. I felt their love and respect in return. It was an incredible feeling. I felt a kinship with each and every one of my guides. I recalled those times in my life when I felt troubled and alone. I would call out to God for comfort. It was then that I would feel a measure of peace and love. I realized it was these precious spirits who comforted me during those times.

My eyes came to rest upon three familiar figures, the swan, the duckling and the frog. The frog held a lily. I smelled its fragrant bouquet.

"Not all of your guides come to you in human form," explained Christopher. "God uses all creation for the messengers of Spirit. Every creature has a purpose. No encounter is coincidental. For a student of God, there is meaning in every moment of life. If only you will open your heart and eyes to see and know. Two doves flying overhead may be bringing you a message of love.

An animal suddenly crossing your path and startling you may be preventing you from harm. When you feel devoid of life, you awaken to the miracle of a budding tree. Most humans are too arrogant to comprehend the pure love of these creatures."

I knew the swan, the duckling and the frog had brought me messages of tremendous importance. I asked Christopher what they were.

"The swan, the duckling and the frog have great wisdom to contribute to your journey home. All will be revealed in due time."

Christopher's eyes shone brightly as he guided me toward the center of the crystal chamber. He admired the precious jewel I held dear. "You have chosen well, Susan. But then you are always divinely guided. There is much to learn from your gem. Place it on the table."

I carefully set the jewel in the center of a table that was illuminated by a shining white light from above and below. I felt tremendous love and energy as my spirit guides surrounded me, coming closer for a better look.

Once again, I saw that the jewel I had selected was composed of three distinct parts entwined as one. Ribbons of different colors merged and mingled in a fluid dance. Each color was magnificent in its own right, but became even richer when blended with the others. The jewel in its entirety was far greater than the sum of its parts.

Christopher spoke with great reverence. "The jewel you have selected contains the secret to fulfilling your destiny in this lifetime."

I didn't understand.

"You have been honored with a great purpose, yet you are not unique. Anyone born during this troubled period of existence has been chosen to complete a crucial mission. Yours can benefit many others, but only if you commit yourself completely to fulfilling your

Divine Destiny. This is not an easy task. Many are called. Few choose to listen. Even fewer have the courage to walk the path, because it is a difficult one, filled with challenges and obstacles."

Christopher studied my jewel carefully. When he glanced back to me, his teal, turquoise eyes were piercing.

"To fulfill your Divine Destiny you must master three key elements entwined as one. Each aspect is difficult in and of itself to understand and master. To fulfill that which you have chosen to accomplish in this lifetime, you are to live a life of Love, Expression and Surrender."

I was disappointed. I thought the magnificent jewel contained secret knowledge, deep mystery, and the key to existence. I had thought I was special. I'd heard the terms love, expression and surrender many times. If all I had to do was master these elements to fulfill my destiny, then my goals were clearly within my reach.

"In theory," said Christopher, "mastering love, divine expression and surrender sounds easy. Living these principles day in and day out is most difficult."

He offered his hand to me. "Come, I will show you."

My eyes remained fixed upon the jewel. Was I to carry it or leave it behind?

As always, Christopher answered that which had not yet been spoken. "Entrust your jewel to Melanie Grace and follow me."

I surrendered the jewel to my guardian angel, then allowed Christopher to guide me. I left the Chamber of Illumination and returned to the interior of the cave. We walked a short distance, then descended a few stairs.

Melanie Grace appeared at the entrance of a narrow corridor. The jewel sparkled in her hands—the ruby circle, the emerald triangle and the sapphire figure-eight, encased within the diamond shell. Suddenly the boundaries of the three distinct shapes dissolved. The figure-eight and the triangle became absorbed as from the center of the radiating colors, the ruby alone emerged.

"The circle—the OM—represents eternity, all that ever was, all that is, and all that shall be. It has no beginning or end. It is eternal and all-encompassing like life itself."

I stepped forward and gazed into the depths of the ruby circle. It no longer looked like a jewel. It was simply substance, with no beginning or end.

"Divine Love is the sum and substance of all that is, the gist of the Creator and of His Creation. It is the essence of this jewel and the essence of you and me, and everything else seen and unseen. Divine Love is the glue that holds the universe together. It is merely the expression of love which takes shape and form."

*M*elanie Grace led us down a narrow corridor alight with a lavender light. But this was no ordinary hallway. Rather, it was a corridor filled with gilded mirrors of different shapes and sizes. I paused in front of the first mirror to my right. Initially I saw only reflective glass. Then slowly an image emerged. It was a face that made me smile—an infant with fine rosy skin and trusting blue eyes. Within the eyes of the baby, I saw all that was pure and good. It was easy to love the innocence of the child.

I gazed left to the second mirror. A different image appeared—the face of an old woman. She had weathered skin and tired eyes. Her eyes were no longer shining with the innocence of the baby. But as I peered closer, I could see a calm knowingness in her eyes. The deep wrinkles etching her face told me she had experienced a life that was neither gentle nor kind. Yet there was a serenity about her that I admired.

The next image to my right was that of a young girl on the threshold of adulthood. She reminded me of my daughter. She possessed great beauty. She embodied all that we value as desirable. The image of the girl with porcelain skin faded, replaced by an equally magnificent mahogany face. Then that image turned into one of an Oriental girl. While marveling at the distinct

beauty God had created within every race and color, I was awed by the brush strokes He used in common.

I was troubled by the appearance of the face in the fourth mirror, a young man somewhere around the girl's age. His face was scarred, and there was anguish in his eyes. Yet deep in his soulful eyes, I detected a glimmer of hope. His face certainly represented the brutality of life—here on earth during these troubled times— but his eyes held a vision that was higher.

I glanced from one image to the next and back again. Each face was unique. Yet, there was a thread in common. What did the faces in the mirrors represent?

"Tell me what you see," Christopher said.

Taking a deep breath, I looked at the faces before me. I examined each one again: the baby, the old woman, the young girl, the scarred boy.

"I see something to be respected and admired in each one. I see qualities which are holy."

"What are they?"

I focused first on the baby.

"When I look at the baby, I see total unconditional love, and nothing but pure potential waiting to be realized. When I look into the eyes of the old woman, I see the wisdom that results from mastering the lessons of a lifetime. Here is a woman who, while having lost the baby's innocence, has experienced all aspects of life and found serenity in the acceptance of it all."

I paused to really study the images of the young girl and the scarred boy.

"The girl represents the beauty of every race. There is brilliance in everyone, to be appreciated when we take the time to look."

The boy's face was the hardest to view, not only because of his disfigurement, but also because of his pain. Yet I saw something there I had to admire.

"When I look in his eyes, I see pain but not despair. I see hope and the possibility of triumph. His ability to seek a higher vision challenges me to do the same."

"When you look at these faces, what do you feel?"

"I feel love."

"So you do," Christopher acknowledged. "Within each person, you can see and feel God's love. Every person whom God creates is a work of art, a unique expression of God. Each life is tremendously valuable. There are no throwaway people in God's Universe.

"You—meaning mankind—spend your life trying to overcome your perceived feelings of unworthiness. Yet by the very fact that you were created, you are worthy. You are divine perfection in the mind of God, or you would not have been created. If you were not—just as you are now—worthy of all good blessings and love, God would have varied His thought of you and created someone else. Don't you get it, Susan? By the very fact that you are alive, you have been chosen. You are right now, in whatever circumstances you find yourself, worthy of your Creator's love and every rich blessing within His Kingdom. How could you ever feel less?

"The life force within each one—no matter how different he or she appears or what experiences they have chosen—is Divine Love, that which we call God. What you see, what you experience of and in each person is God."

Christopher took my hand and gently led me even farther down the corridor where Melanie Grace stood before another large gilded mirror. Melanie Grace moved to my right while Christopher stood on my left. The mirror was dark.

"Let's see where the face of God appears next," he said.

I glanced to the floor then back again. A hazy image slowly appeared. As the image sharpened, I became aware of another face. It was that of a toddler, not yet two. But this child was no stranger. I recognized the cherub cheeks, the pug nose, the mischievous brown eyes. The baby's face in the mirror was mine.

Slowly the first image faded as another took its place. This image was not nearly as captivating as the small child was. Painfully I saw myself as an overweight thirteen-year-old, with pigtails and horn-rimmed glasses. A familiar feeling of loathing came over me. I still carried the image of that awkward adolescent deep within my buried place of scars.

The next image was that of a young woman who'd finally found herself. The awkward girl had become a woman. My appearance was much more pleasing, but my eyes were filled with insecurity.

The final image was my face as I appear now, a mature woman of forty. It was painful to view myself as I really am, with wrinkles and imperfections. I waited for the image to fade, but the picture remained.

"Don't focus on the facade. Look deep in your eyes. Glimpse your spirit, the real essence of you."

I stepped closer.

"See what God sees."

Taking a deep breath, I acknowledged one of the most difficult challenges I'd ever faced. I'd spent a lifetime merely accepting what others saw as the true reflection of me.

Closing my eyes, I prayed. "God, let me see myself as you do."

When I opened my eyes and looked up into the face I knew to be my own, I saw an entirely different image. I saw myself with the unconditional love of the newborn baby. I saw the wisdom of the old woman. I saw the beauty that was uniquely me. Deep within my eyes, I beheld a vision of a higher good not yet experienced, of potential as yet untapped. I saw in my own face the qualities I had seen in the baby, the old woman, the young girl, and the scarred boy. For the first time, looking at myself, I saw God. I felt love.

I stood in silence as quiet tears ran down my cheeks. After a time Christopher said, "You've seen the face of God in humanity. You've even recognized Him in yourself."

He guided me down the corridor to the last set of mirrors. "Can you see God in these faces?" he asked.

One by one, familiar faces appeared in the mirrors to my left and to my right. These faces did not make me smile. These were people from my present and my past.

"It's easy to see the Divine in people you love. It's much harder to recognize God in the ones you loathe."

Even though I'd left it at the entrance of the cave, I instinctively reached for my knapsack of baggage, where I carried these very images with me always as reminders of hurt and regret, buried anger, past mistakes.

"Look at them, Susan. Each and every one. Take your time. Study them carefully. You cannot move forward until you get beyond the past."

The first image I had to confront was that of my husband. If not for him, I wouldn't be here. Looking at his reflection, my stomach began churning. I recognized the feeling as anger. I blamed him for causing our lives, like the tin plane, to spin out of control. Other members of my family began appearing. I realized then some of the petty resentments I clung to, even with the daughter I so dearly loved.

One face began merging into another ... people I thought I'd forgotten ... from my childhood and my youth through adulthood. Each one represented something different—betrayal, disappointment, lack of love, fear. I confronted my past relationships one by one. I thought I was a woman who forgave easily. The images staring at me, together with the feelings that stirred, proved me wrong.

I looked deep into the eyes of those who disturbed me. Some were images of people I still held dear, but many were the faces of those I'd hoped to never see again. Yet a most amazing thing happened. As I looked, really looked, at each one ... I saw a reflection not of them ... but of me.

"Think of creation as a giant triangle, like the emerald within your jewel. God, as the Source, gives that which He is equally to all. Now invert the triangle so that all that was created is funneled back in kind to the Source, to the beginning point. What do you have but the Creator?"

I realized in that moment a profound truth. "You're saying that we're all one. That which is me is you, and that which I call you is the same as me."

Christopher nodded. "God created each one of us to be an expression of Himself. In truth, each and every person is simply a different expression of the same thing ... that which we call God ... that which we know as Divine Love. Each person is a different reflection of the other."

"Then why are we so disturbed by the actions of others?" I asked.

"Look in the mirror, Susan. That which you see in another is merely a reflection of yourself—be it what you like or what disturbs you. People are brought together during their lives to express what God is ... pure unconditional love. Oftentimes we fall short of the mark in truly expressing God."

I knew what Christopher was saying was important. I wanted desperately to understand. "What do you mean?"

"We are all created in the image and likeness of God. That which God is, we are. We are the expression of God in physical form. But we have free will. We choose how we wish to express God ... or not. Oftentimes we don't express our highest potential. We miss the mark. We err. We judge others as good or evil, their actions as right or wrong. We are judged in return. But look again into the faces of those who have been brought to you. Tell me what you see. Tell me then what you feel."

This time as I gazed into the faces of those from my past, I felt compassion and understanding. I remembered the sadness and disappointment I'd felt when not living up to my potential, when treating others as less than I wished to be treated. This time when I looked at their faces, I remembered what I'd learned from every one. I realized in that moment that I was who I was, what I was, and where I was because of them. Had it not been for each person from my past presenting me with challenge and learning, I would never have reached the point where, crashing into the sea of despair, I'd journeyed home.

I turned to Christopher in awe. I could find no words to speak.

"Give thanks to those who have brought you here. Without them, you would not be the person you are. They are part of you. They have made you strong. What you saw in their eyes was indeed a reflection of yourself. Some qualities you have chosen to retain, other qualities you realize no longer serve you. Your knowledge of yourself increased, your love of self deepened because of your experiences together. That which you termed pain was really growth. What you gained from these relationships— through all the pain and the sorrow—were greater pieces of yourself."

This time when I looked at all the faces from my past, I saw myself. And I liked what I saw—beauty, wisdom and triumph.

"What do you see?" Christopher asked. "What do you feel?"

"I see God. I feel love."

"Well done, Susan. You are ready to proceed."

At the far end of the corridor, just beyond the mirrors, was a door. It began to open slowly.

"Now that you've realized the truth of your past relationships, you may have your knapsack returned if you like."

I looked at Christopher with wide eyes. "Why would I want it back?"

The door swung open. There in the center of yet another room was a huge bowl of fire. Suddenly my knapsack appeared in Christopher's hands.

"The past no longer is. Yet, because you have free will, you can choose to retain all the hurt and the anger from the past. Or, you can understand and bless your past, then release it."

"How do I do that?" I asked.

"You release your past by choosing to forgive the judgments you've held about yourself and others. You retain the knowledge that you've gained, but you release all those you've held in bondage together with the anger and the hurt."

"I'm ready. Tell me what to do."

"Let go of the vestiges of the past that no longer serve you. Cast your anger and resentment into the burning flame, there to be purified by the fire and returned to the ethers for new creation. Bless all those who have served you. Release them into the hands of the Creator. See the highest good now for all concerned."

Christopher placed the knapsack in my hands. I walked to the burning bowl, bowed my head, and committed my past to the flames. I released all those people I'd held in bondage and blessed all the situations in my life that had brought me here.

I uttered my own version of a well-known prayer. "Father, forgive me for my judgments and my anger. I didn't know what I had done."

"The Creator holds no judgment. God sees only your highest potential, that which He created you to be ... that which He is ... and you are. That is the holy vision held for all."

Stepping back, I watched the knapsack engulfed by the fire. The flames danced with delight. The ashes rose from the fire there to be carried on the wings of angels into the ethers.

"What happens now?" I asked.

"The ashes—wisdom gained from lessons mastered—are consumed by the Universe and transmuted into the good that shapes your future."

"How do I keep from filling up another knapsack with garbage? It's second nature to judge ourselves and others."

"You realize that everyone you encounter is simply a mirror, showing you aspects of yourself to better know and understand. Likewise, you remember that everyone is of God—no matter what his or her actions. Some choose to express their highest potential. Others, unfortunately, do not. Bless with compassion those whose choices are not the highest. They will continuously be shown mirrors of themselves until they choose a better way and a higher vision.

"People have no concept of the divine plan for their lives. Your soul seeks constant evolution. Chosen ones appear on your path to bring you greater awareness of yourself in relationship to your Divine Destiny. But rather than gently releasing these beloved ones when the growth has been accomplished, you hold on for dear life in the name of obligation."

Christopher smiled. "Imagine the walk of life as a never-ending adventure filled with delight and wonder. Along the path you encounter a sandbox. You join others in the sandbox for a while to play, but there comes a time to move on. Rather than gleefully accepting the wonder of the next encounter, you grow afraid of the unseen lurking around the next bend. You refuse to leave the sandbox, even though you find your playmates no longer enjoyable. The fine grains of sand suddenly turn into little balls of glue. There you remain stuck with those whom you choose not to release. You can't move forward. You feel frustrated and stuck. Sound familiar?"

I laughed at Christopher's analogy of a child's game. How many times had I chosen to remain in situations with people long past time simply because I lacked the courage to move on?

Christopher paused and glanced away, calling to mind another image. "Think of a leaf, now withered and brown, that refuses to surrender gracefully and fall from the branch. It clings on tenaciously through the winter until spring, when the new bud

bursts forth and the smothering leaf is cast off. How much easier the process would have been if the dying leaf had simply let go and freely moved on with its evolution. Life will evolve with or without your cooperation. It's up to you whether you participate freely through graceful surrender, or wait until the inevitable forces of life launch you into your next stage of growth."

*H*aving fully let go of the shackles of the past—the judgments, resentments and anger—through the mighty power of release and purification, I was free. My breathing had slowed. I was calmer. The heaviness I felt weighing me down had lifted. I felt lighter, even brighter. And yet without the familiar burden of the illusions I had created and the negativity I held dear, I felt a frightening void.

"Don't give in to the fear, Susan. You are ready to move beyond the past and create a rich, new present. The void will be filled with purpose and direction."

With Christopher on my left, and Melanie Grace—cradling my jewel—to my right, we left the Chamber of the Burning Bowl. We walked a short distance and then ascended three stairs into a lovely, circular room. The room radiated soft hues of azure, turquoise and lavender. It was a tranquil room, but the energy surging about was electrifying. I felt the anticipation of new beginnings. I couldn't wait to see what was going to occur next.

Christopher and Melanie Grace led me to the front of the room where three plush chairs were situated before a huge motion picture screen. Melanie Grace turned and, without uttering a word, carefully placed the jewel in my hands. The circle, the triangle, and the figure-eight design within the diamond were once again clearly and distinctly visible. And yet there seemed to be no boundaries between the gems. Their energies were totally blended.

Christopher invited me to be seated in the middle chair. Melanie Grace sat to my right, Christopher to my left. My guide and my guardian angel bowed their heads in prayer. I joined them, expressing my gratitude to a loving God who had delivered me to a place of rapture and peace. I wasn't sure what was to come, but I'd never felt such excitement.

The circular room began to fill with my spirit guides and teachers. I was enveloped in an energy field of pure love.

Christopher said, "You have now walked through the Corridor of Mirrors. You have glimpsed God in the faces of humanity. You have acknowledged the Presence within yourself. You have learned the powerful secret of forgiveness. You have recognized that each person is a mirror, through whom to realize more of yourself with love and acceptance. You have discovered that freedom comes from realizing your growth and releasing your past, rather than clinging to anger, resentment and fear."

I nodded. The words he uttered were true.

"Now, having freed yourself from the glue of the past with the void created by release, you are ready to re-create your world by discovering your true purpose for incarnating this lifetime. This is a powerful moment. Are you ready?"

"I am, Christopher. I've been waiting years to understand my true purpose."

"Everyone is born with the seed of fulfillment carried deep within their heart. Life is a process of discovering the self and your true purpose for being. God has a magnificent universe created to support you with your mission. To understand the process, we must recall the initial lesson in the Corridor of Mirrors. God is the Source of All. We are the expression of God in physical form. We are here to discover more about ourselves, hence more about God, all the while expressing God's love to creation.

"When conceiving you in the Divine Mind, God, while sourcing you with *all* of Himself, blessed you with a *particular* aspect of the divine to express. Your unique talents are gifts from your Creator. You have been charged with a duty to share those talents and gifts with your fellowman in your own special way."

As I was cradling my jewel, a most amazing thing happened. The jewel with the three distinct shapes entwined as one changed form yet again. The circle and the figure-eight became absorbed as, from the center of the gem, the triangle alone emerged.

Christopher directed my attention to the viewing screen. The first image that appeared on the screen was a huge triangle just like the one I held in my hand. At the top of the triangle the word *God* appeared. At the point, bottom left, was the word *Susan*. Following the line to the opposite point, there was written the word *Mankind*.

"God, the Source of All, blesses you with aspects of Itself that distinguish you as an individual expression of God. You, in turn, are challenged to share these God-given talents in service for the betterment of others. When you do this to the best of your ability, and someone is uplifted, they in turn give praise back to the Source for their creation. The triangle is completed.

"The world exalts those who seem exceptionally gifted, such as a composer or artist. But the truth is that everyone has been blessed with certain gifts. It is a matter of discovering those gifts and sharing them freely with others. The teacher who lights a passion for learning in a student, the counselor who helps the addicted stop the abuse of alcohol or drugs, the one who feeds the hungry, shelters the homeless or gives the downtrodden a reason to live, are as great and magnificent in the eyes of the Creator as the composer and the artist.

"Remember that we each have a piece to contribute to God's Mosaic. Each piece—when fully realized—is a work of art. No part is greater or less than any other. But it takes the expression of each shared gift to create the masterpiece God envisioned as humankind."

"How do we discover our special gifts?" I asked.

"The answer is incredibly simple," Christopher said. "You begin by asking yourself what brings you joy."

"Joy?" I repeated.

"Do you have any idea what joy is?" he asked.

"It's the feeling of being happy," I answered.

"It's so much more than that. Happiness is an illusive quality you seize from time to time when things go well—someone does what you want, or you acquire a new possession. Joy is the sense of being fully alive that comes when you feel connected to God and His Universe. You experience true joy when you are sharing the essence of your being and your talents with God's magnificent Creation. So begin to discover your God-given talents by asking what you do that creates joy."

The movie screen came alive with images, like a home movie of myself as a young child.

"Spirit gives you many clues along the way. God wants you to succeed and to fulfill your Divine Destiny this lifetime. Look at yourself, Susan. What are you doing?"

In the first scene I was about eight years old. From the time I was old enough to play outside, I organized my little friends into a theater troupe. We'd act out skits and plays, sometimes even musicals. Watching the scene, I could trace my love of acting and music to our backyard theater productions.

In the next movie I was ten years old, delivering a neighborhood newsletter that I wrote and sold for a quarter. I was thirteen in the next scene. I had written a play for my eighth-grade class.

"What do you see?" Christopher asked.

Shaking my head in amazement, I answered, "I see myself doing then what I love doing now: writing and performing."

"That's right," Christopher said. "Some people know from early childhood what special talents they possess or what they love to do. Look back to the games you played as a child. See the free spirit you were back then before you became so concerned with words like obligation and security."

"I know what you're saying is right for me, but does everyone glimpse their gifts as children?"

"No," Christopher said. "Some children are not blessed with the freedom to explore in their youth. The lessons of their childhood are much too harsh. Yet still, they encounter teachers who see their potential or parents who recognize and encourage their God-given talents.

"Some people have to wait until adulthood to evaluate their lives to see what their gifts really are. Again, they must ask themselves what brings them the greatest joy.

"The Creator wants us to live joyfully and fulfilled in every moment. That is the purpose of Creation. So when we are expressing joy, we are fulfilling the intent of the Creator. When we—through the expression of our unique talents and gifts—are expressing God in service to mankind and experiencing joy, we know we are fulfilling the Divine Destiny of our lives. That's the road map to heaven."

"But Christopher, there's something I don't understand. I recognize the value of one whose talent might be the preparation of a lovely meal for someone in need. That service will produce joy in the moment. But what if the expression of someone's gifts takes years to achieve? What then?"

Christopher's lips curled under in amusement. "How do you write a novel?" he asked.

"I write a novel one page at a time."

"Must you wait until the completion of the last page to feel joy?"

"Oh no!" I answered emphatically. "Unless I enjoyed the process, I could never complete the work. It's much too difficult."

"So be it with life. Life, to be experienced fully, must be lived one moment at a time, being keenly aware of every blessing, every joy, and every encounter in the moment. Even if you are a most skilled craftsman, the only way to build a path is one brick at a time."

"So it's possible to experience joy in the process of expression?"

"It's absolutely essential," he replied.

I remained silent for a time. There was something else that puzzled me.

"All right then, what's the missing piece? I am doing what I love to do. I write books. I am expressing my gifts and talents. I enjoy the process of writing. So why don't I feel fulfilled?"

"Think about the triangle, Susan. God has blessed you with the ability to write and to communicate. You are writing, that's true. But are you sharing your talent with mankind? What are you doing to benefit others?"

I paused, taken aback.

"The key to experiencing lasting joy is to share your gifts with others. Are you using your communication skills in service to God? Are you helping others to write or to publish? Are you helping young people discover their dreams and live to their potential? Are your books meant to uplift others or only to benefit you?"

My cheeks grew warm. I was getting angry. Justifiably so, I thought. "But I have to earn a living!"

Feigning a measure of disappointment, Christopher said, "Has this entire pilgrimage been for nothing? Think back to the beginning of our journey home. Remember the island, Susan?"

My thoughts returned to the image of me standing alone in the center of a desolate island, being pummeled by wind and rain, my clothing torn in shreds, my food spoiling. "Oh yes," I said. "I remember."

"What did you learn from that experience?"

"I learned that by our own wits, we can survive for a time. We are a resourceful people, whether living on a desert island or in the midst of a city jungle. But sooner or later when fueled by our need for power and control, unexpected events occur and we become vulnerable to forces much greater than ourselves."

Christopher stood. "There is a better way," he said.

We left the projection room and walked down a long, narrow corridor in silence. Suddenly a huge door swung open and we walked outside. The air was crisp and cool. The sun was shining brilliantly. I shielded my eyes for a moment against the bright light. I was surrounded by a field of emerald green abounding with beautiful flowers growing wild. The beauty of the field astounded me.

"Look around, Susan. Tell us what you see."

"I see a field rich with soil and grass. I see flowers growing everywhere. I hear the birds. I feel the sun. Everything is perfect, in complete order."

"God supplies the needs of everything that He has created in full measure. Like a parent providing for a treasured child, so you are indulged. When you are expressing God in service to mankind, the Creator provides everything and everyone needed to prosper you."

Together we walked through the beautiful field of spring.

"There is a plan for every expression of life. The seed of fulfillment is contained within each tiny bud, each blade of grass. The Creator utilizes all creation for the benefit and growth of every other life form. The potential of the spring flower is nurtured in the ground by the decay of the falling leaves. So you are nurtured as well, even during those dark gray times you call the winter of your life. The seeds of your new beginning are taking root.

"The Creator knows your every desire and the perfect timing for its fulfillment. The Creator holds the master plan for His Creation, not you."

"Should we pray then?"

"You have no idea how to pray."

"What do you mean? I pray all the time."

Christopher's smile was indulgent. "See this with the humor that we do. You look around the playground of your life. Rather than appreciate the vastness of your blessings, you notice only the lack of what you don't have. Then you write a grocery list to God, detailing what you want. You regard God as the delivery boy. You become impatient when your sacks of abundance are not delivered exactly as you ordered and on your time schedule. You curse God and doubt His existence.

"Think about the spring flower. During the dark days of winter, you yearn for the rich color and fragrance of the spring flower. You desire spring with all your heart. If the Creator brought forth your desire before its natural time—even though your desire is a good one—the beauty of the spring growth would be destroyed by the cold winds of winter. But in due time, spring bursts forth. It's worth the wait. The Creator knows His Creation, all aspects of His Creation, best. So it is with you. Stop and give thanks. Your life is filled with abundance, if only you would pause long enough to see. Accept life as it is and as it isn't in this moment. Savor the gift of life you've been granted. Give thanks with joy, for all things are working together—even though you don't always see—for the ultimate fulfillment of your Divine Destiny."

"Is it all right, then, to ask for what we think we need and desire?"

"Of course it is," Christopher replied. "True desires come from that gentle place in the heart that often heralds the next stage of your growth and expression. A woman who yearns for love may be ready to embark upon her path to union. She should become ready by learning how to love herself and others more fully. She must not become despondent, though, when daylight descends into darkness and the one she seeks has failed to appear. She should live her life expressing God, trusting completely that at the exact moment that divine timing is right, she will meet the one she is to romantically love."

Inhaling the cool, crisp air, my guide smiled. "There's a secret to life and to praying that few people practice. Remember: Many are called, few choose, and even fewer have the courage to walk the path."

I was intrigued. "What secret, Christopher?"

"If what you desire is love, then give thanks for love in your life. Don't limit your prayer to the manifestation of romantic love. Seek the richness of love and relationship in all aspects of life. Give thanks for the gift of love expressing in your life, no matter what form it takes. Then give away in rich measure that which you desire. If you seek love, then give love with all your heart and being. If you seek money, pause and savor the abundance in all areas of your life without limiting the form. Watch for the miracles. Give away that which you desire. Give to others freely of your talents and your treasures."

He continued. "If you seek health, then give thanks for life. Look around and see where life abides. Connect with all forms of life. Choose to live fully in the moment. Cherish yourself as the Creator cherishes you. Take care of yourself by making life-nourishing choices. Exude the essence of life—your being—to others. In other words, Susan, to have more of what you want, recognize and accept what you do have, give thanks for your blessings, and give away that which you desire. That's the secret to praying."

Christopher knelt down in the field of green and plucked a single blade of grass.

"Pray with an open and grateful heart to God. Your prayers are delivered on the wings of angels. Thank God in advance for the fulfillment of your dreams. Then trust that your prayers will be answered. Everything that you require to fulfill your Divine Destiny will be manifested in due time. Be willing to stand tall like the blade of grass, savoring the experience of life and giving thanks to the Creator for your blessings. Don't waste a moment of your precious life yearning for what you think you lack."

Christopher tickled my cheek with the blade of grass.

"Your life will become a series of miracles. As you express God in service to others, watch how you meet exactly the right people at the precise time to aid you in the process."

Christopher savored the beauty of the resplendent field, then once again beheld me.

"When you dedicate your life in service, you no longer need to make a living. There is no finer employer than God. The Creator will see that you are richly blessed with creative ideas, opportunities, and the means to prosper you. Most particularly the Creator will see that you are richly blessed with the precious commodity that everyone desires but no one has enough of ... and that is what you have been desiring all along ... joy."

"Our time together is drawing to a close," Christopher said. "Walk with us through the field."

In silence we meandered through the sumptuous field of grass and wildflowers. I walked between Melanie Grace and Christopher. All my teachers and guides followed. I felt tremendous love as I enjoyed the fullness of life with my wonderful companions. I didn't want this time to end. I didn't want to leave my friends.

After a time, we came to a mighty river. There perched on the banks was a sturdy canoe. The rugged craft was adorned with the same magnificent jewels that I'd seen inside the sacred cave of my soul.

"It's time to take what you have learned here and return to the physical place you previously called home. But before you go, there's yet another aspect of your jewel to master."

Melanie Grace stood before me, cradling my precious gem. Yet again, the three distinct shapes merged and a single gem emerged from the center. It was the sapphire figure-eight.

I watched with fascination as the gem began changing its shape and form. Its path became neither linear nor circular. Rather, the lines curved and crossed. There was no constant pathway from one point to the next.

"Life was never meant to be clear-cut and predictable," said Christopher. "Rather than being boring, life is meant to be filled with spontaneity and surprise. Life is not stagnant. It is in a constant state of evolution. The only thing that is predictable about life is that nothing remains the same. So it is with you and the process of living."

Christopher led me toward the canoe.

"Everyone is born with a blueprint for the fulfillment of their Divine Destiny. When you surrender with love to this divine plan, your life is filled with glory and wonder. It doesn't mean that there won't be obstacles, but you will be guided through every challenge with the understanding that all things are working together for your ultimate good."

Three of my spirit friends joined Melanie Grace to stand before me. They were the swan, the duckling and the frog.

"Your friends have come to deliver their message."

The swan and the duckling turned to face each other.

"Remember the lesson from the Corridor of Mirrors. What we see in one another are really aspects of ourselves. We are all created of and by the same Source. The swan sees the duckling as a creature of unlimited, untapped potential. The swan blesses the little fellow on its path to becoming more than it dreamed possible.

"The duckling sees the swan as dreams realized. The duckling thrills to what it might become. Both the duckling and the swan treasure the same aspect of each other, and that is divine potential."

The duckling, with its scraggly black feathers, stepped forward and saluted me.

"The duckling wants you to truly see the beauty in all of God's creatures."

The swan turned and inclined its head majestically.

"The swan asks that you surrender to life as it does, with grace and beauty."

The frog stepped forward holding a lily.

"What is the frog's message?" I asked.

"The frog is considered a lowly creature. Yet its croak is clearly discernible. The frog wants you to know that your message, like his voice, is a message that can be heard by all. The wisdom of your jewel—fulfillment of your Divine Destiny through a life of love, expression and surrender—is for everyone, no matter his or her creed or religion."

The frog offered me its lily. It was a beautiful white flower. The intricacies within the center of the lily were fascinating. I felt a tremendous wave of peace as I held and beheld the flower. I knew it had great meaning.

"The lily's meaning for you is twofold. The lily represents the Christ Self of you, the Divine Essence of God that you and everyone else simply IS. In addition, the name Susan means lily. So for you, this flower also represents that which God is expressing through and as you. When you are attuned to the true nature of your being and expressing that which you are, you are as complete in your unfoldment as this precious lily."

I accepted the lily with honor. I thanked the frog, the swan and the duckling for their messages. I knew it was time to return

to the life I had known. Yet I knew my life would never be the same.

As I neared the canoe, a thought stopped me. I remembered my meditation just before journeying to the cave. I realized how important every aspect of the meditation had proved to be. From my guardian angel watching from above, to the duckling, the swan and the frog. There was one other figure who'd appeared in the meditation, but whose role we'd not yet discussed.

"What about my husband?" I asked. "Why was he a part of that picture?"

"When you centered yourself and went within to that quiet place where the journey home begins, what did you see?"

"I was seated in a gondola in tranquil waters."

"Who was at the helm?"

"My husband was," I replied.

"That's right. By allowing him to pilot your boat, you had relinquished your personal power to your husband. In other words, Susan, you were allowing him to guide your life ... not your spirit."

Christopher took my hand and led me to the sturdy canoe encrusted with jewels.

"Now it's time to be the master of your own destiny. Your dreams are your road map, but true mastery comes from surrendering control to Spirit. By climbing into the boat of surrender, with full faculty and thought, you are agreeing to allow the destiny of your life to unfold through love and expression in God's perfect time and way. Are you ready to surrender control to Spirit?"

I nodded, then I took a deep breath and centered myself. I closed my eyes and prayed.

"Dear God, I surrender my life to You. I desire only to be an expression of You in the fulfillment of my Divine Destiny. My life is Yours. Your everlasting life is mine."

As I opened my eyes, I felt a sense of calm and peace that I had never known.

"Remember that the ride will not always be smooth. The currents of life are often like treacherous waters. Sometimes the ride of surrender is peaceful, while at other times you will think that your boat is filled with holes. You'll be required to hold onto your faith for dear life. Are you willing to accept the totality of the ride?"

I remembered the last time I'd heard Christopher utter this same invitation. I was drowning in the sea of despair. He piloted the lifeboat. He asked me then if I was sure I wanted to take the ride. Little did I know what he meant then. I could only guess what he meant now.

With all the sincerity in my heart, I said, "Yes, Christopher. I gladly accept the ride."

I started to climb into the boat. A thought stopped me. I looked at Melanie Grace cradling my beautiful jewel.

"What happens to my jewel now?"

"The essence of the jewel remains with you—inside of you—because it is you. But with your permission, Melanie Grace will deliver this symbol of you, this jewel, to God to hold as your commitment to seeking mastery in this lifetime."

I felt deeply blessed as I prepared for the next phase of my journey. I gazed at the wondrous lily symbolizing first the divine

expression of God within all of us—the Christ consciousness—and the particular talents and gifts of God as individually expressed by and through me, a woman by the name of Susan.

Gently I handed the precious lily to Christopher.

"Would you keep the lily for me?" I asked. "Would you hold the vision of what I am and what I can become?"

"It would be a privilege to do so, Susan."

Christopher offered me his hand and helped me into the canoe.

"Where do I go now?" I asked.

"You return to your life in the present moment exactly where you are. I will meet you there. Remember as you surrender to the Divine Destiny of your life, to always leave a wide berth for surprises. Trust in the process of living and surrender. Seek always to express that which you are with love and in service."

I didn't bid good-bye to my spirit friends because I realized that they would always be with me. Christopher pushed the canoe into the water with a mighty shove. And I was off, navigating the currents of the flowing river, holding on for dear life. In virtually the next instant, I was standing in front of the house I had left behind, the place I had called home.

Everything seemed exactly as I remembered. Nothing had changed. Through the living-room window I glimpsed my husband

and my daughter. I wondered if anyone realized I had nearly drowned in the sea of despair before being rescued and taken on a journey far beyond my wildest imagination.

As I walked up the brick pathway leading to my front door, I felt trepidation. I didn't know what I would find inside. I knew that while nothing might appear different on the outside, everything had changed inside of me. By accepting my mission—the fulfillment of the Divine Destiny of my life—nothing could remain as it was.

Christopher was waiting for me in the front yard. There was a mischievous grin on his face. His hands were concealed behind his back.

"I have gifts for you, Susan, to remind you of our time together." Opening his right hand, he presented me with a tiny mustard seed. "This is to remind you that within the seed of every dream is the potential for its ultimate fulfillment. Plant your dreams with faith."

I accepted the mustard seed as my new beginning. I couldn't wait to plant it.

Christopher then revealed the treasure he concealed in his left hand. To my amazement it was the same leaf, the color of a golden sunset, that I had watched falling from the maple tree outside my living-room window. It was the dance of the leaf that showed me I was living a life devoid of joy.

"Treasure the leaf always, Susan. Never forget, during those times you experience as death or change, that there is always new life being created. It is the dying leaf that blankets the incubating seed. Trust the process of life."

Christopher bowed to me graciously. I knew this journey was finished ... or perhaps merely beginning.

"I have a final secret to share with you," he said. "When you surrender to the Divine Destiny of your life, living fully in the moment through love and expression in service, there are no more scripted dramas. Rather, life becomes a symphony."

I felt the presence of my loved ones—those in physical and those in spirit form—all around me. Feeling their love was like a celestial symphony filled with unity, harmony and peace. Melanie Grace appeared. Joining hands with Christopher and me, we began moving together in a slow splendid dance.

Dear reader, do you hear the music of Spirit?

Come home and dance with the angels

where the music never ends.

To order additional copies of
"Dancing with Angels"
or
To arrange speaking engagements
with Susan M. Hoskins

Contact:

Integrity Press, Ltd.
P.O. Box 8277
Prairie Village, KS 66208
Phone: (913) 642-4100
Toll Free: 1 (888) 860-2535
Fax: (913) 642-4214

e-mail: integritypress@sprintmail.com

Other books by Susan M. Hoskins:
"Twisted Lights" (suspense novel)
"Twisted Secrets" (suspense novel)